CUSTER

To Custer and Minto
whose story echoes the lives
of two who went before . . . .

CHOCKY AND BLACKIE

And a special thank you
to Kimmie, owner of Minto, for all
her help in the making
of this book.

CUSTER

The true story of a horse

Deborah King

RED FOX

DEEP IN THE HEART of the countryside on a farm tucked away in the trees, there lived a young colt, the son of Cotton Lord, the most magnificent stallion in the county. The farmer was very proud of his young horse, and he called him General Custer after the famous cavalry officer noted for his courage and strength.

But this particular Custer had no great ambitions. He preferred to take life easy and spent his time roaming with the cattle, doing all the things that cows do.

Almost all! When the cows were being milked, Custer was busy thinking about the most important thing in his life – his stomach. For Custer, no food was too difficult to reach, and he soon found a way of opening the door to the farmhouse kitchen and helping himself. Eventually he grew so fat that he couldn't even squeeze himself through the doorway. Something would have to be done. So, with a heavy heart, the farmer sold him to a riding school where he would learn how to be a proper horse.

But Custer learned very little. His new companions were not at all friendly. Even the small ponies bared their teeth and lashed out at him with their hooves, and he ran away whinnying for his friends the cows. After all, he thought he *was* a cow, and he had been very happy being a cow and he didn't want to be a horse at all.

During the cold winter, Custer walked alone. He wandered about scuffing his hooves, his head hanging low and a faraway look in his big, sad eyes. His coat grew dull! It was nothing like the rich chestnut of his father's. It was pale and shaggy and his mane stuck up on end. Worst of all he had been given a new name – Cowardy Custard!

The school could do nothing to lift his spirits. He felt abandoned and forgotten.

But at last, someone from the nearby village took pity on him, and in the spring he was moved to a new home by the sea. He had a stable of his own and lots of good food which he learned to share with a new family of animals. But Custer didn't really belong.

During the long dark nights he pined for his real family – the herd of cows.

One misty morning, Custer stepped out of his stable to find that he was not alone. In the far corner of his field stood a strange and beautiful creature.

A wild grey mare was hiding in the hedgerow. Her name was Minto and she had been captured from her home in the depths of the forest and sold at market. She was safe now. Her life had been spared but, still terrified by her ordeal, she stood there shaking and trembling with fear. Custer kept his distance, careful not to frighten her.

At dusk she was put into a stable next to Custer. But warmth and comfort meant nothing to Minto. She was a wild horse used to sleeping out in the open. Throughout the night she kept Custer awake with the frantic pacing of her hooves as she tried to break out.

Custer became restless and anxious. Somehow he understood that she was a creature who needed to run free.

Unlatching the stable doors with his teeth, he released her into the night. But for Minto, even this was not enough. She looked longingly to the hills beyond and before he knew it, Custer had untied the field gate and was racing after her across the heath. They galloped far away, up and over the hills.

Dawn came and the two horses were still running. Minto raced with the wind as if to shake off the memory of her capture and imprisonment.

But as she reached the clifftops, she stopped. She looked out across the sea. Here was more wildness than she had ever known, even in the forest.

In a second Custer was off again. Now he would take the lead and show Minto the open spaces where she could run free. As he galloped with her he began to understand what it meant to be a horse.

He stayed close, whinnying softly to warn her when danger was near and nuzzling her gently to reassure her. Slowly, she grew calm and began to trust him.

And as the day drew in, Custer set off down the beach for home knowing that she would follow.

The villagers had been out all day searching for the two horses, and there was a joyful welcome awaiting their return.

Everyone noticed the difference in Custer. He walked with a spring in his step, his head and tail held high. After all, he had new responsibilities. It was to be a new life for Minto, and he must help her to adapt. But no one could hope to tame Minto's spirit. She even taught Custer the ways of a wild horse. How to gallop like the wind and buck like a bronco.

In return, Custer showed Minto some of the benefits of human friendship. In time, she lost her fear and began to settle into her new home and a new life with Custer.

By the end of the summer the two horses were inseparable – no one could part them now.

When winter came round again, Custer and Minto were moved to a new field with a wood of tall trees for shelter. It was like Minto's forest home, but set high on a hill overlooking the cliffs and the open sea.

As for Custer, he finally lived up to his name. With the silver mare at his side, he had grown into a strong and powerful palomino with a coat that shone like autumn gold. Even the General would have been proud of him.

And each day at dusk, a long line of cows would slowly wind its way
down the hill to the dairy. Custer would look up and sigh deeply.
All that seemed *such* a long time ago.

A Red Fox Book

Published by Random House Children's Books
20 Vauxhall Bridge Road, London SW1V 2SA

A division of Random House UK Ltd.
London Melbourne Sydney Auckland
Johannesburg and agencies throughout the world

First published by Hutchinson Children's Books 1991

Red Fox edition 1993

5 7 9 10 8 6

© Deborah King 1991

The right of Deborah King to be identified as the author and
illustrator of this work has been asserted by her in accordance
with the Copyright, Designs and Patents Act 1988.

Printed in China

RANDOM HOUSE UK Ltd Reg. No. 954009

ISBN 0 09 974570 4